WHAT'S WRONG?

Anna Pomaska

DOVER PUBLICATIONS, INC.
Mineola, New York

Bibliographical Note

What's Wrong? is a new work, first published by Dover Publications, Inc., in 1997.

International Standard Book Number: 0-486-29563-X

Manufactured in the United States of America
Dover Publications, Inc., 31 East 2nd Street, Mineola, N.Y. 11501

Lillie and Logan are baking cookies.
They are so busy that they don't see
7 wrong things in the kitchen.
Can you find them?

Gordy and Sara are enjoying their picnic,
even though 6 odd things are happening.
Can you find them?

Find the 6 things that are wrong in this picture
of Lisa feeding the chickens.

3

Bobby and Leslie are having a crazy lunch.
Find the 7 things that are funny.

There are 6 things wrong in this picture of Steve
and Elaine skating on a cold winter day.
Find the 6 odd things.

This is a picture of a silly street.
Do you see the 7 things that are silly?

More silliness on the street! Can you see
the 5 things that are really crazy in the picture?

Things look a little funny to Anna
after visiting the toy store.
What are the 6 things that are wrong?

There are 6 funny things happening
in this picture of Tina under the apple tree.
Can you find them?

What are the 7 silly things that are happening in this picture?

Matt likes to build snow men in the winter,
but things have gotten very mixed up.
What are the things that are wrong in the picture?

The children are being taught to read and write.
They are not aware of 6 things that are wrong around
them. Can you find the things that are not right?

There are 6 things wrong in this picture of Jesse playing his flute in the park. Do you see them?

Amy is giving her horse an apple but there are
7 strange things in the picture. What are they?

14

Hallie is at home reading, but 6 things
are very weird. What are they?

Eric and Victoria are washing the car, but 6 strange things are happening. Do you see them?

Barbara and Tommy's house is very unusual.
Can you find the 5 strange things?

Nancy is skipping rope in front of her house.
She does not notice 6 unusual things around her.
Can you see them?

Do you know which are the 7 wrong things in this picture of George and Mary around a campfire?

It is a beautiful sunny day at the beach
and Megan is playing in the sand.
What are the 5 things that are wrong?

Find the 5 things that are wrong in this picture of Maria building a sand castle at the beach.

There are 5 things that are strange in this picture.
Can you find them?

Lillie and Logan are picking apples to bake
some pies. They do not notice 5 strange things
around them. Can you see them?

GROCERY

If you look and read carefully you will find 9 things that are wrong here.

24

Sally is a very strange skier. Find the 5 things
that are odd in this picture.

Janet loves to dive beneath the sea.
She expects unusual sights, but 6 things do not
belong here. Can you find them?

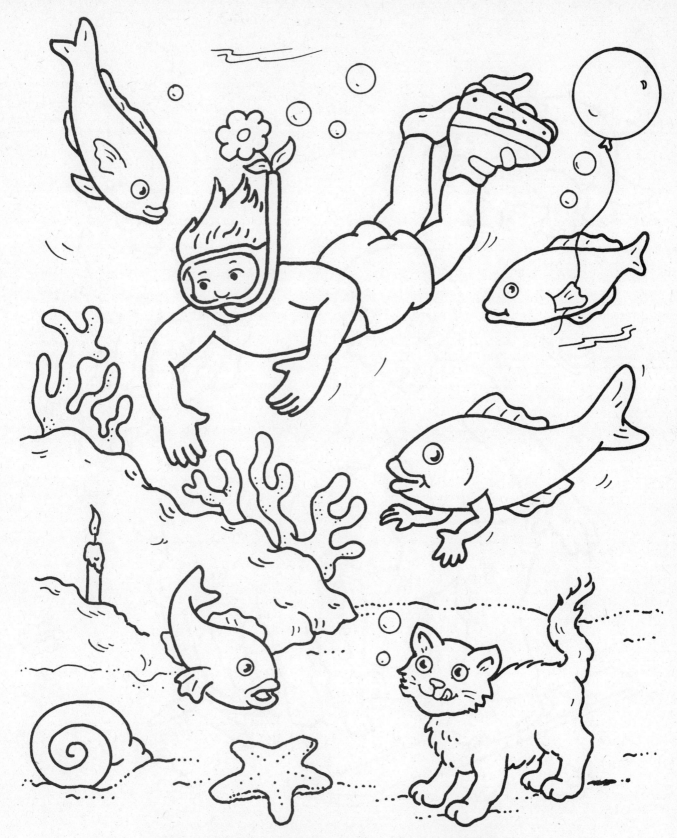

Chuck loves to go snorkeling,
but today he is seeing some very strange things.
What are the 6 things that are wrong?

David likes to visit and pet the lamb
in the meadow. He does not notice that 5 things
are very odd. Can you see them?

Tommy and Alice are working in the garden but there are 7 things wrong. Can you find them?

Is Lisa dreaming or are there really 6 weird things happening in the night?